POCKET
SPACE

© Catherine Barr 2019

Catherine Barr has asserted her right to be identified
as the author of this work.

Published in October 2019

A catalogue record for this book is available from the British Library

ISBN 978 1 78521 671 8
Library of Congress control no. 2019942914

Design and layout by Richard Parsons

Published by Haynes Publishing,
Sparkford, Yeovil, Somerset BA22 7JJ, UK
Tel: 01963 440635, Int. tel: +44 1963 440635
Website: www.haynes.com

Haynes North America Inc.,
859 Lawrence Drive, Newbury Park, California 91320, USA

Printed in Malaysia

The author would like to thank Steve Williams for valued advice.

The following agencies have given permission to use their images:
NASA Image and Video Library: pp10, 14, 15 top, 20, top, 23 centre and bottom left, 26, 27, 35 top, 36, 38, 40, 41, 42 bottom, 54–55, 56, 57 bottom, 61 top,
62, 63 top, 64, 65, 67, 73 bottom, 81, 85 bottom, 87 bottom, 88, 89 top, 90–91,
100, 104, 105 right, 107, 120, 122, 123, **Alamy**: p52, 53, 61 bottom, 93 bottom,
95 top, 103, 108 top, 111 bottom, 126 top, 127 top, **Getty**: pp: 111 top.

The Author

Catherine Barr writes nonfiction stories to spark curiosity and conversation. Her first
book, *The Story of Life*, was shortlisted for The English Association Picture Book
Award and was followed by *The Story of Space* and *The Story of People*. She has
also written books with the Natural History Museum where she worked, following
years as an environmental activist, when she star gazed from Greenpeace boats.

POCKET MANUAL
SPACE

Haynes

CONTENTS

INTRODUCTION
THE BIG PICTURE

People have always dreamed of space. Early humans gazed up at African skies. They hunted under the sun and slept under the stars. Our ancestors and people ever since have puzzled over our place in the universe. By staring at the skies, using maths, inventing telescopes, sending spaceships and finally sitting in rockets and living in orbit, we have learned a lot. We humans are endlessly curious. We know that space is amazing and that it is still the biggest mystery of all. In this book, you'll glimpse what we know about space. In chapters that spin outwards from planet Earth towards deep space, you will see the big picture and wonder about the mysteries that remain.

The book is divided into chapters that look at different aspects of space in turn. These include:

> The solar system
> Stars and constellations
> Galaxies
> The universe
> Space mysteries

But first, let's put space into perspective…

DID YOU KNOW?

There may be 100 billion galaxies in the universe. Earth lies in the Milky Way, the milky streak that you can see stretching across the night sky...

INTRODUCTION
SIZE IN SPACE

Finding out about space is difficult, mostly because it is SO big. It is bigger than you can possibly imagine. Everything in space is a long way away from everything else. In fact, everything is so far apart in the universe that scientists invented a new way to measure the greatest distances in space. This measurement is called light years. One light year equals 9.6 trillion kilometres!

GIANT FACTS

- A light year is the distance light travels in one year. Our nearest star, Alpha Centauri, is more than 4 light years from Earth.
- It would take 200,000 years at the speed of light to cross our galaxy, the Milky Way (if that were possible...).
- Although the planets would fit between Earth and the Moon – that's actually 'very close' by universal standards!
- Scientists think our universe may be infinite, which means it might go on forever.

Alpha Centauri

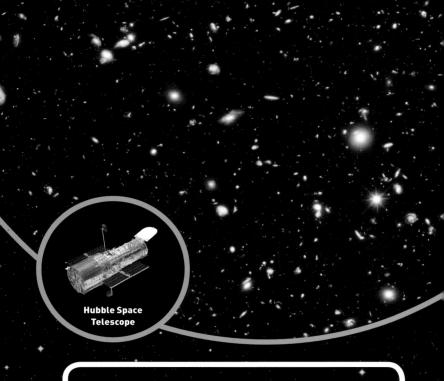

Hubble Space
Telescope

DID YOU KNOW?

The 'observable' universe that scientists can see
with telescopes, like the Hubble Space Telescope,
is 13.8 billion light years away from planet Earth.

EARTH IN SPACE

Earth is a pale blue dot in space. Our planet is just a speck of light in a black universe. It can be seen here in this famous photograph taken by spacecraft *Voyager 1* on 14 February 1990. It was taken from 6.5 billion kilometres away, right at the edge of the solar system. *Voyager 1* has since left our solar system and is now headed into deep space.

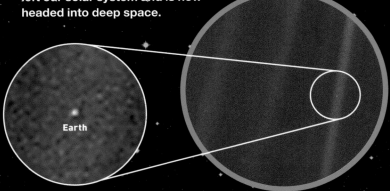

Earth

'Look again at that dot. That's here. That's home. That's us. On it everyone you love, everyone you know, everyone you ever heard of, every human being who ever was, lived out their lives.'

CARL SAGAN, COSMOLOGIST, *PALE BLUE DOT*, 1994

BLUE MARBLE

The first picture that showed Earth as a globe was taken by the Apollo 17 crew on 7 December 1972, as they left Earth's orbit for the Moon. Earth's deep blue oceans and swirling clouds make it look like a blue marble in space.

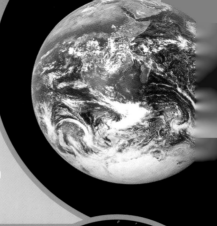

EARTHLY FACTS

- Like other planets, Earth is round because gravity pulls it into a ball shape.
- Earth is spinning so fast that our globe is squashed at the poles and swollen at the equator.
- There are more than 500,000 pieces of tracked 'space junk' orbiting Earth, but looking at Earth from afar, they are too tiny to show up.

LIFE IN SPACE

As far as we know, Earth is the only planet with life. But it is unlikely that in the entire universe our planet is the only place where life exists. For this reason, space scientists are trying very hard to find evidence of other forms of life.

THE FOUNTAIN OF LIFE

Water is needed for life as we know it and our planet is unique in having oceans of surface water. Earth looks like a blue marble from space because of blue seas that swirl around the globe. The only known life in the universe probably began deep in these huge oceans. Like all other forms of life on Earth, we humans evolved from this extraordinary watery beginning 3.8 billion years ago.

> Earth lies in the 'Goldilocks Zone' – just the right distance from the Sun for the temperatures to make liquid water on our planet's surface possible.
> The diversity of life on Earth is amazing! More than 8 million named species of life have evolved on our planet.
> Places in our solar system that might host life include Saturn's moon Titan and Jupiter's moon Europa.

DID YOU KNOW?

Water has been found on other planets and moons in our solar system but is locked in ice or is deep below the surface. Scientists are investigating whether or not these secret water stores might also have the right conditions for life or even contain the ingredients for some form of life.

INTRODUCTION
SCIENCE IN SPACE

S pace scientists from all around the world are working together on Earth and up in space to collect and share information, news and photographs of the universe. We are entering a new Space Age of knowledge, discovery and potential for space science, exploration and even holidays in space!

WORKING IN SPACE

The International Space Station (ISS) is a busy science research station in low orbit around Earth. Since 2000, it has been home to a permanent crew of up to six astronauts who are stationed there for six-month-long missions. There, they carry out all sorts of experiments in space science and technology.

UNMANNED SPACECRAFT

Unmanned spacecraft go into space without people on board. Controlled from Earth, they send information back for scientists to study. Unmanned space missions range from the rovers on Mars to spacecraft making fly-bys of the giant gas planets, probes landing on comets, and *Voyager 1*, which was the first spacecraft to reach interstellar space.

GIANT TELESCOPES IN SPACE

Launched in low orbit in 1990, the Hubble Space Telescope is one of many gigantic telescopes in space: it is the size of a large school bus. Powered by the Sun, it takes amazing pictures of distant stars and galaxies that help us to understand the universe and learn more about space.

LIVING IN SPACE

On 20 July 1969, American astronaut Neil Armstrong took 'one giant leap for mankind' as he stepped on to the Moon. This remains the only time that humans have ever stood anywhere else in the universe apart from Earth. In the next decade, space scientists plan to put people on Mars, to see if it is possible to live beyond Earth.

Neil Armstrong, 1969

SPACE TRAVELLERS

> People who are trained to pilot and crew spacecraft are called astronauts.
> It takes many years to train to be an astronaut and you need to be super fit!
> Over 550 people so far have rocketed into space.
> 220 astronauts from 17 countries have worked on the International Space Station.

PACE HOLIDAYS

here are plans
o put a space
otel into orbit.
he company who
wns it will then be
ble to offer a luxury
pace experience to
olidaymakers.
ompanies around the
orld are already
king bookings for
olidays in space.
pace tourists may
op the Moon,
xperience zero
ravity and get a
unning snap of
anet Earth.

DID YOU KNOW?

In low orbit, you'll whizz around Earth
at 28,150 kilometres per hour every 92
minutes, seeing up to 16 sunrises and
sunsets every 24 hours!

OUR SOLAR SYSTEM

In our galaxy alone, there are more than 2,500 stars with orbiting planets. Explore our own very special solar system...

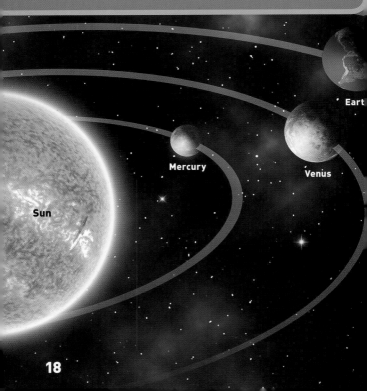

Sun

Mercury

Venus

Eart

Uranus

Neptune

Jupiter

Saturn

Mars

DID YOU KNOW?

Our solar system used to have nine planets, including an icy ball called Pluto. But in 2006 scientists voted, controversially, to knock Pluto off the planet list because it was too small. Pluto is still spinning beyond Neptune but is now called a dwarf planet.

THE SPIN

1. GETTING STARTED

The solar system began with spinning clouds of dust and gas. Around 4.5 billion years ago, these clouds swirled so fast that they began to shine and our yellow Sun was born.

2. THE PLANETS ARE CREATED

Leftover particles of dust and gas bumped and clumped together, eventually forming the four small rocky planets closest to the Sun: Mercury, Venus, Earth and Mars. Far away from the Sun's warmth, four gigantic gas planets formed: Jupiter, Saturn, Uranus and Neptune.

3. ASTEROIDS AND COMETS

Circling space rocks and ice eventually formed dwarf planets, moons, rings, asteroids and comets orbiting the Sun.

> Billions of potato-shaped space rocks make a belt of asteroids spinning between Mars and Jupiter.
> Broken bits of asteroids and comets make up the spectacular rings of Saturn.
> Trillions of comets or 'dirty snowballs' fly towards the Sun from the Oort Cloud, a ring of icy objects that scientists believe circles the far reaches of our solar system.

DID YOU KNOW?

That 'shooting stars' are the streaks of light in the sky caused by space rocks called meteroids burning up as they enter the Earth's atmosphere and become meteors.

A SPECIAL STAR

Our Sun is 4.5 billion years old. It is a shining ball of gases that makes up 99.8 per cent of the mass of the whole solar system. It is the Sun that makes life possible here on Earth. Like every star, one day the Sun will die. It is now halfway through its life. Humans may not be around, but in 5 billion years it will swell into a gigantic ball of red gas and engulf our solar system!

Sun spots

The Sun's surface has shifting dark spots called sun spots. These darker patches are places where the surface is less hot than the overall super scalding temperature of 5,500 degrees Celsius.

Sun light

It takes 8 minutes and 20 seconds for sunlight to reach Earth.

Solar flares

Supersonic solar winds explode and loop out from the surface of the Sun. The flashing curtains of northern and southern lights, called auroras, are caused by solar winds that reach Earth and clash with our planet's magnetic field. The auroras are seen where the magnetic field is strongest, towards the North and South poles.

THE PLANETS

Mercury 'Swift planet'
- Speedy orbit but a slower spin than Earth
- Burning hot in the day and freezing at night
- A dusty grey brown surface of craters or 'wrinkles'

Earth 'Blue planet'
- The only planet with water on its surface
- In the 'Goldilocks zone' just the right amount of light and heat for life from the Sun

Closest to the Sun

Venus 'Earth's evil twin'
- Scorching hot with a thick, choking atmosphere of cloud and acid rain
- Below the yellow clouds it has a black barren surface of solid lava flows

Mars 'Red planet'
- Dry, dusty red surface with dust storms
- It has two moons
- Its Mount Olympus is three times as high as Everest

Saturn 'The Jewel'
> Giant gas planet with rings of rock and ice
> Has ferocious winds and storms
> Has 53 named moons… One, Titan, has the only atmosphere of any moon in the solar system

Neptune 'Big blue'
> There may be an ocean of super hot water under its cold clouds
> Has supersonic winds

Furthest from the Sun

Jupiter 'Giant planet'
> Monster hurricanes. The great red spot is a storm so big that Earth could fit inside it
> It has 79 moons… some have oceans beneath their crusts that could support life

Uranus 'Ice giant'
> The coldest planet, made of gas and ice
> Spins on its side, probably tipped over by a collision

25

OUR SOLAR SYSTEM
CLOSE TO THE SUN

Although Mercury is closest to the Sun, and has more extreme temperature ranges than any other planet, it is not actually the planet with the highest temperatures in our solar system. The thick atmosphere on Venus, second closest to the Sun, traps the heat, and this greenhouse effect means that Venus is the hottest planet.

Surface of Mercury

Mercury

Mercury is covered in craters and many of these are named after famous artists, musicians and writers including children's author Dr Seuss.

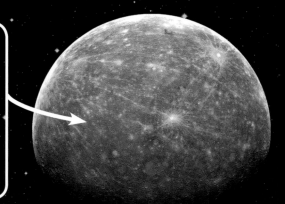

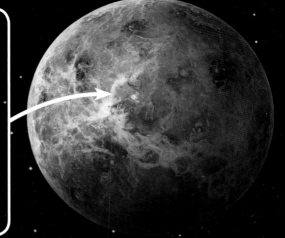

Venus

The second planet from the Sun and the third brightest object in Earth's sky after the Sun and Moon. It is sometimes referred to as the sister planet to Earth, because their size and mass are so similar.

ROCKY FACTS

> Venus spins in the opposite direction to most planets
> More than 40 spacecraft have explored Venus
> The surface of Venus is hidden by clouds
> Many scientists believe there was once water on the surface of Venus
> Venus is named after the Roman goddess of love and beauty

Alpha Region, Venus

OUR SOLAR SYSTEM
OUR HOME

Earth is the only place we can be sure there is life of any kind. So as far as we know, only humans on Earth are lucky enough to look up and see spectacular sights in the night sky. People have wondered at space since ancient times but now we are learning to understand what we see.

AURORAS

At the poles, our atmosphere lights up with amazing curtains of lights called auroras, flashing across the skies. They are caused by solar storms looping out from the Sun and meeting the Earth's magnetic field. These natural light shows are called the Northern or Southern Lights, depending on whether you are looking up in the northern or southern hemisphere.

SOLAR ECLIPSE

When the Sun, the Moon and the Earth line up across space there is a solar eclipse. The Moon blocks the Sun's light and casts a shadow on Earth.

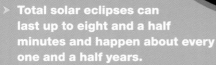

➤ Total solar eclipses can last up to eight and a half minutes and happen about every one and a half years.
➤ There are two other different types of solar eclipse: a partial eclipse and an annular eclipse.
➤ A lunar eclipse occurs when a full Moon passes behind Earth into its shadow.

DID YOU KNOW?

Depending on the geometry of the Sun, Moon, and Earth, there can be between two and five solar eclipses each year.

SPACE JUNK

Earth's orbit is littered with space junk, made up of bits of launch debris, abandoned spacecraft and other leftovers from space missions. In total, there are over half a millions bits and pieces of junk flying around, presenting a growing problem to space flights and safety. Of these, more than 20,000 are bigger than a football. Space agencies are trying to track these larger bits of junk so they know where they are and can hopefully avoid collisions that could damage or harm space missions.

How small?

Because they are travelling so fast, really tiny pieces of space junk – even flecks of paint – can damage spaceships.

How fast?

Bits of space junk are dangerously whizzing around in orbit at 28,150 kilometres per hour, risking serious crashes with satellites and spacecraft.

Cleaning up

There are lots of ideas for how to clean up this space litter. From pushing it out of orbit into deep space to sweeping it up with gigantic space nets, space engineers are working on all kinds of engineering solutions to mop up the mess.

OUR SOLAR SYSTEM
MOONS

Moons are space rocks in all shapes and sizes that orbit planets or asteroids. There are more than 190 moons in our solar system, a few of which have atmospheres. Some have hidden oceans. Scientists think that some moons may even have the right conditions for extraterrestrial life.

EARTH'S MOON

Earth's Moon formed when a gigantic rock smashed into our planet and a chunk of rock was knocked off into space. Pulled around by gravity, this new space rock became our familiar Moon. But on the Moon itself gravity is very weak, as Neil Armstrong discovered when he stepped on it in 1969. Because there is no wind on the Moon, his footprints are still there!

GALILEAN MOONS

With 79 moons, the planet Jupiter has more moons than any other planet in the solar system. Four of these, the Galilean moons, were first seen in 1610 by the astronomer Galileo Galilei. Io, Europa, Ganymede and Callisto are all very different. Europa has more water than Earth and scientists think it may have the right conditions for life.

MOON FACTS

> Saturn's largest moon is named Titan. It is the only moon known to have a dense atmosphere.
> Neptune's largest moon, Triton, is similar in size to Earth's Moon. Discovered in 1846, it is the seventh largest moon in the solar system.
> Mars has two moons named Phobos and Deimos. Both were discovered in 1877.
> Venus and Mercury have no moons.

MARS

Known as the 'red planet' because of its blood-red dusty surface, Mars is dry, rocky and icy cold. It has the largest volcano in the solar system, polar ice caps and weather. Like Earth, it rotates on a tilt so it has seasons too. Expeditions to Mars have discovered that, long ago, Mars was once much wetter and warmer and may even have hosted forms of life.

Life on Mars

Humans are making plans to live on Mars. It will be an exciting adventure but Mars won't be a cosy, comfortable home. Unlike Earth, the atmosphere is mostly carbon dioxide, gravity is weak and it's very cold indeed. So astronauts will need to live inside a 'habitat bubble' in which they can breathe, grow food, study space and keep warm.

Sunset and sunrise

During the day

Red and blue sky

From the surface of Mars, the red dust makes the sky look brownish-red during the day, while at sunset and sunrise it is a cool blue around the Sun.

MARS FACTS

> If the ground shudders on Mars, it might be a Marsquake.
> There are snow flurries on Mars ... but not enough to build a snowman.

JUPITER

It's no secret that Jupiter is the largest planet in the solar system. But this description really doesn't do it justice. For one, the mass of Jupiter is 318 times as massive as the Earth. In fact, Jupiter is 2.5 times more massive than all of the other planets in the solar system combined.

Great Red Spot

The Great Red Spot on Jupiter is one of its most familiar features. This persistent (it never stops!) anticyclonic storm, which is located to the south of its equator is the most gigantic storm in the solar system.

Inside Jupiter ...

... there may be deep oceans of a strange metallic liquid that doesn't exist on Earth.

JUPITER FACTS

> The swirls and stripes on Jupiter's surface are cold windy clouds of ammonia and water.
> Nine spacecraft have visited Jupiter.
> Jupiter does have rings but they are too faint to see.
> Jupiter has a powerful magnetic field.

Spinning around

For all its size and mass, Jupiter moves super quickly. In fact, with a rotational velocity of 12.6 km/s (~7.45 m/s) or 45,300 km/h (28,148 mph), the planet only takes about 10 hours to complete a full rotation on its axis. And, because Jupiter spins so rapidly, the planet has flattened out at the poles a little and bulges at its equator.

SATURN

Like Jupiter, Saturn is a gas planet so it doesn't have a solid surface. But below its swirling yellow clouds, it has layers of unearthly liquids that may surround a rocky or even a liquid core.

Saturn's rings

There was a time when Saturn was without its rings. The latest findings suggest they formed during the age of the dinosaurs on Earth, 10 – 100 million years ago. The rings are made up of cosmic objects ranging from icy slithers to mountain-sized lumps. Sometimes, Saturn's rings are fully open, and we see them in all their glory, but other times when we see the rings edge on – it looks like they've disappeared.

Spinning around

Determining the rotation speed of Saturn was actually very difficult to do, because the planet doesn't have a solid surface.

SATURN FACTS

> Is so light that if you could pop this giant gas planet in water it would float.
> It has a unique polar jet stream with 200 mile-an-hour winds.
> It has only been visited four times by spacecraft.

Rings C and B close up

The rings are named alphabetically in the order they were found... the main rings are A, B and C.

ICE WORLDS

At the edge of the solar system are Uranus and Neptune, the most distant planets of all. These are known as the ice planets. Scientists believe that diamonds fall like raindrops towards the centre of these ice-cold gas spheres, which spin so far away in the dark.

Uranus

Uranus is tipped over on its side with an axial tilt of 98 degrees. It is often described as rolling around the Sun on its side. No other planet spins with such a tilt. It rotates the opposite way to Earth and most other planets.

Neptune

Neptune is the furthest planet from the Sun but strangely not the coldest... This is because there may be an ocean of super hot water beneath its clouds.

CHILLY FACTS

> The gas methane that swirls around both ice giants makes Uranus look blue-green and Neptune look darker blue, further from the Sun.

> Neptune's clouds are whipped around by the strongest winds in the solar system.

> They are so far away that they have only been visited by one spacecraft, *Voyager 2*.

Clouds on Neptune

BELTS & CLOUDS

There are three astronomically big bands of rocks and ice in orbit in the solar system. Swept around by gravity, billions of different shapes and sizes of rock and ice form the Asteroid Belt, the Kuiper Belt and probably the Oort Cloud, far out towards interstellar space.

ASTEROID BELT

> Most asteroids orbit the Sun in the space between Mars and Jupiter.
> Space rocks in the Asteroid Belt are leftovers from the formation of the solar system.
> Ceres, the largest asteroid, is 476 kilometres in diameter!
> The Asteroid Belt is 1 astronomical unit (AU) thick (see page 46).

Ceres

KUIPER BELT

The Kuiper Belt is much bigger than the Asteroid Belt and lies at the outer edges of the solar system. It's thought to stretch across 20 AU of space. It is also made up of space rocks of all sizes in a region beyond Neptune. There are estimated to be trillions of comets in the Kuiper Belt.

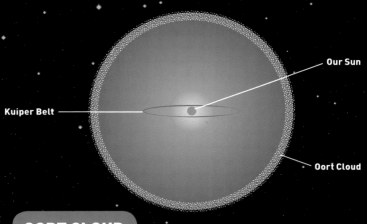

Our Sun

Kuiper Belt

Oort Cloud

OORT CLOUD

This shell of icy objects, like comets, is believed to lie about 2,000 AU from the Sun in the outermost reaches of the solar system. There may be more than a trillion objects spinning in the Oort Cloud. No one has ever seen it but scientists believe that the Oort Cloud exists.

 # SPACE ROCK

WHAT IS AN ASTEROID?

A small rocky object orbiting the Sun. Some are dwarf planets while others are just chunky space rocks.

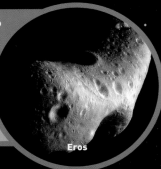

Eros

WHAT IS A COMET?

A small cosmic object made up from ice and dust. When comets orbit close to the Sun, ice melts and a white 'tail' of gas and dust streams away from the object. There are over 3,500 known comets, some are as big as a small town!

Dust tail
Curves slightly in direction of orbit

Coma
Gas and dust

Gas tail
Points directly away from the Sun

Nucleus
Ice and rock

METEOROID, METEOR OR METEORITE?

> A meteoroid is a bit of rock that may be part of a comet or asteroid travelling through outer space.

> A meteor is the streak of light you see when a meteoroid zooms through Earth's atmosphere and burns up. Most disintegrate and break up but some reach Earth.

> A meteorite is a lump of space rock that actually crashes into Earth. Less than 5% of meteorites actually reach the ground. But if you find a small, shiny, fist-sized rock somewhere, it might just be part of a meteorite.

A giant meteor

DID YOU KNOW?

Around the time life first formed, there was a heavy bombardment of meteorites smashing into the planet. They formed what are now some of the oldest rocks on Earth.

45

OUR SOLAR SYSTEM
HOW BIG?

Distances in space are so enormous that they are difficult to imagine and even more difficult to measure. For this reason, scientists have invented different measurements for space so that the numbers don't get too big. These include astronomical units and light years.

ASTRONOMICAL UNITS

An astronomical unit (AU) is about the distance from Earth to the Sun, which is 150 million kilometres. Scientists use astronomical units to measure the distances between objects like the Sun, planets, asteroids and comets. Mars is 0.52 AU from Earth (or 225 million kilometres), while Jupiter is 4.2 AU from Earth.

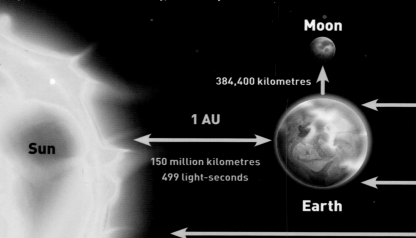

Moon

384,400 kilometres

1 AU

Sun

150 million kilometres
499 light-seconds

Earth

THE EDGE OF THE SOLAR SYSTEM

The distance from the Sun to the inner edge of the Oort Cloud in the far reaches of the solar system is 1,000 AU. The outer edge of the Oort Cloud may be 100,000 AU away. The edge of the solar system is the region in space where the Sun's gravity is no longer strong enough to pull objects around in orbit.

KILOMETRES

For much closer objects, like the distance from Earth to the Moon, the distance is measured in kilometres. The Moon is about 384,400 kilometres away.

LIGHT YEARS

A light year is the distance travelled by light in one year: 9.7 trillion kilometres. Scientists use light years to measure the distances beyond our solar system.

Jupiter

0.52 AU or 225 million kilometres from Earth

Mars

4.2 AU from Earth

The distance from the Sun to the edge of the solar system is 100,000 astronomical

TIME TRAVEL

Earth takes one year to orbit the Sun. Other planets in our solar system take different lengths of time, which means the length of year varies from planet to planet. Closer to the Sun, a year is shorter than it is on Earth, and on the planets furthest from the Sun, a year is really long.

DID YOU KNOW?

Venus spins so slowly on its axis that one day on the planet lasts nearly 243 Earth days. Because it's closer to the Sun than Earth is, the planet has a 225-day year. So, the day is actually longer than a year, which means if you were on Venus you would only see two sunrises each year.

ALL IN A YEAR

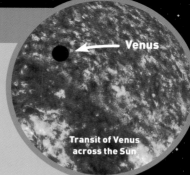

Venus

Transit of Venus across the Sun

> A year on Mercury is 88 Earth days (0.2 years).
> A year on Venus is 225 Earth days (0.6 years).
> A year on Earth is 365 days (1 year).
> A year on Mars is 687 days (2 years).
> A year on Jupiter is 12 Earth years.
> A year on Saturn is 30 Earth years.
> A year on Uranus is 84 Earth years.
> A year on Neptune is 165 Earth years.

ALL IN A DAY

> A day on Mercury is 1,408 hours.
> A day on Venus is 5,832 hours.
> A day on Earth is 24 hours.
> A day on Mars is 25 hours.
> A day on Jupiter is 10 hours.
> A day on Saturn is 11 hours.
> A day on Uranus is 17 hours.
> A day on Neptune is 16 hours.

Sunrise on Jupiter

CAN I SEE IT?

WITH YOUR NAKED EYE

You can see much of the solar system with your own eyes. If you know when and where to look in the night sky, on a clear night you can easily find the five brightest planets: Mercury, Venus, Mars, Jupiter and Saturn.

> You can only see one moon with your naked eye: Earth's Moon.
> Neptune is the only planet that you can't ever see with your naked eye.
> You can see stars in the Milky Way in interstellar space, and even spot the galaxy Andromeda as a white smudge in the distant sky.
> You can glimpse the bright flash of the International Space Station whizzing by if you know when to look.

Saturn

Antares

Venus

WITH YOUR BINOCULARS

You can get a much closer look at planets and even other galaxies through binoculars. You can explore craters on the Moon and even spot the four Galilean moons of Jupiter.

WITH YOUR TELESCOPE

You can see the ice giants Neptune and Uranus at the outer edges of our solar system and even focus in on a distant comet or an asteroid.

WHAT IS A TELESCOPE?

A telescope is a magnification tool. Using one is the best way to investigate the sky because it will allow you to see distant objects more clearly. With the most gigantic, very powerful telescopes, space agencies spot distant galaxies in deep space and take amazing pictures.

SOLAR SCIENTISTS

ARISTOTLE

Aristotle was born in Ancient Greece (384–322BC). He is famous for being a great thinker and scientist but he wrongly believed that the Earth was at the centre of the solar system and that the Sun orbited the Earth.

NICOLAUS COPERNICUS

Nicolaus Copernicus was born in Poland (1473–1543). He is an astronomer famous for working out that the Sun is actually at the centre of the solar system and that the planets orbit the Sun.

JOHANNES KEPLER

Johannes Kepler was born in Germany (1571–1630). He is famous for working out how the planets moved around the Sun. He realised that the Sun's gravity pulled the planets around in orbit – in ellipses (ovals) rather than perfect circles.

GALILEO GALILEI

Galileo Galilei was born in Italy (1564–1642). He is famous for being a great thinker, astronomer and mathematician who made an amazing telescope and used it to discover the four biggest moons of Jupiter, as well as the rings of Saturn.

CAROLINE HERSCHEL

Caroline Herschel (1750–1848) was a German-born British woman who became the first professional female astronomer. She was the first woman to discover a comet and be awarded a prize by the Royal Astronomical Society (1835).

THE STARS

Astronomers believe our Sun is just one among 100 billion stars in the Milky Way. Discover the colourful lives of stars scattered across the universe...

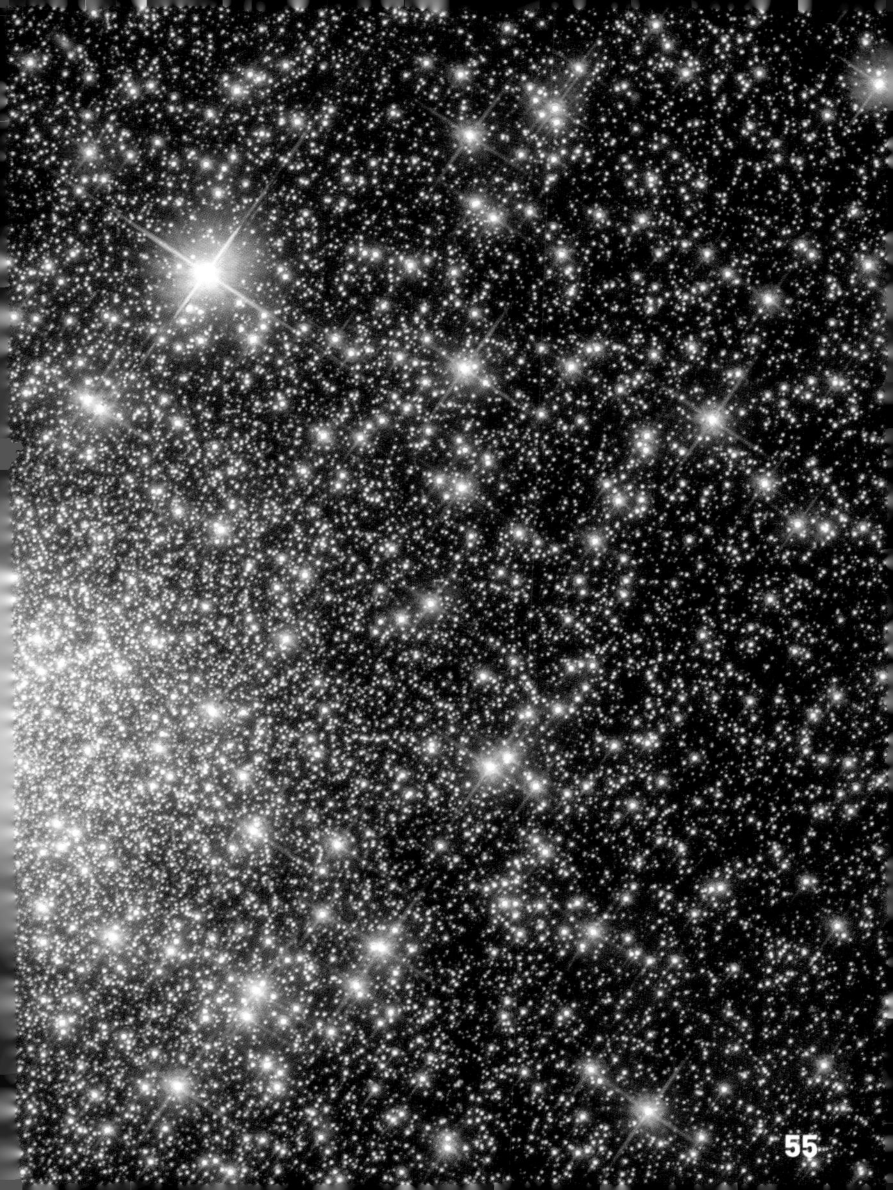

SHINING STARS

A STAR IS BORN

Stars are born, live and die. In the early universe, it took 180 million years for the first stars to shine. Now there are more than 1 billion trillion stars glittering across space.

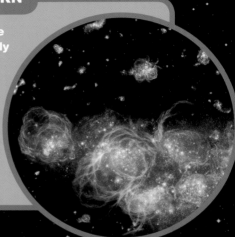

DID YOU KNOW?

Billions of stars are born each year in the whole universe of 100 billion galaxies. But the number of stars born is falling: 95 per cent of all stars that will ever live have already been born!

WHY STARS SHINE

Cold clouds of the simplest gas in the universe, hydrogen, swirl into tighter and tighter balls. As gravity spins this gas it heats up. Over millions of years, as the temperature soars, a new gas called helium eventually forms. The creation of helium causes a massive explosion of energy that makes stars glow and shine with light. The Sun's light energy makes all life on Earth possible.

HOW STARS DIE

Hydrogen is the fuel that keeps stars burning. When stars run out of hydrogen, they begin to die. Some blow up and explode in a spectacular final burst while others simply fade away into the mysterious blackness of the universe.

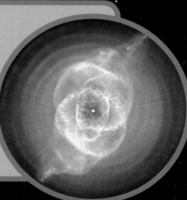

COLOURFUL STARS

I t might not look like it from Earth, but stars come in rainbow colours, depending on how hot they are. All stars are very hot, but different colours show just how hot each one is.

The H-R diagram

Astronomers plot stars according to their colour and brightness. This graph shows the brightness and temperature of different stars. It is called the Hertzsprung–Russell (or H–R) diagram. Most stars, like the Sun, are on the 'main sequence' with plenty of fuel to burn. When they run out of fuel, they can become cool, red giants or dim white dwarfs, depending on their mass.

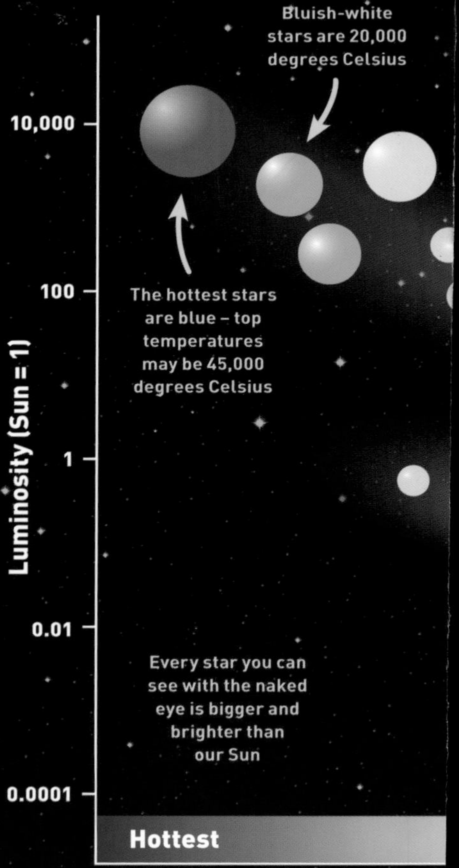

Bluish-white stars are 20,000 degrees Celsius

The hottest stars are blue – top temperatures may be 45,000 degrees Celsius

Every star you can see with the naked eye is bigger and brighter than our Sun

Luminosity (Sun = 1)

10,000

100

1

0.01

0.0001

Hottest

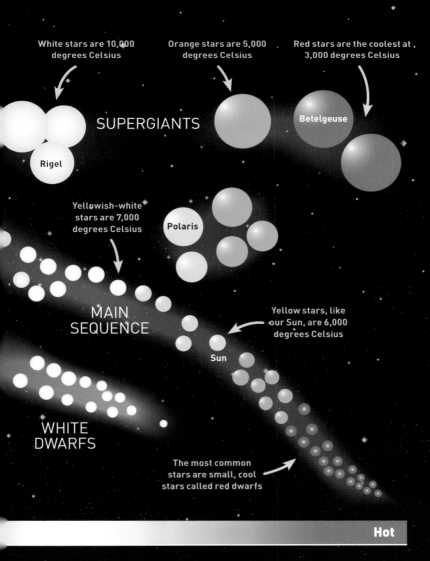

White stars are 10,000 degrees Celsius

Orange stars are 5,000 degrees Celsius

Red stars are the coolest at 3,000 degrees Celsius

SUPERGIANTS

Rigel

Betelgeuse

Yellowish-white stars are 7,000 degrees Celsius

Polaris

MAIN SEQUENCE

Yellow stars, like our Sun, are 6,000 degrees Celsius

Sun

WHITE DWARFS

The most common stars are small, cool stars called red dwarfs

Hot

SUPER STARS

THE SUN: OUR CLOSEST STAR

> This 'ordinary' star provides all the energy and light that make life possible on Earth.
> The Sun is our closest star, so it is the most studied star in the sky.
> It has a mysteriously super hot upper atmosphere called a corona, which glows around it.
> Supersonic solar winds flare out from the Sun's surface.

DID YOU KNOW?

The Sun is about halfway through its life... One day it will run out of fuel and swell up and cool down into a massive red giant. It will engulf Mercury, Venus and probably Earth too, but not for about 5 billion years so there's no need to worry!

BETELGEUSE: RED SUPER GIANT

> This gigantic red giant star is 10 million years old.
> It's big and burning fast so could explode at any time as a supernova.
> It is more than 500 times bigger than the Sun.
> Find it in the constellation of Orion. It is above the equator, which means that you can see it from both the northern and southern hemispheres.

Betelgeuse

POLARIS: YELLOW SUPER GIANT

> This North Star is directly overhead at the North Pole.
> It's a bright supergiant that you can see from Earth.
> It is famous for guiding sailors due north while at sea.
> Find it in the constellation of Ursa Minor in the northern hemisphere.

Polaris, surrounded by star trails

STAR SYSTEMS

Most stars spin in pairs. These binary stars have a dimmer companion or sometimes more than one companion star. The brightness of some stars changes and they flicker in the sky. These are called variable stars.

SIRIUS: BRIGHT BINARY STAR

> The brightest star in the sky – Sirius blazes 20 times brighter than the Sun.

> It's known as the Dog Star because it's found in the constellation Canis Major or Big Dog.

> Sirius flickers in different colours, so it is also known as the rainbow star.

> It spins with a companion – a smaller, dimmer star called Sirius B.

> It is 8.6 light years away from Earth.

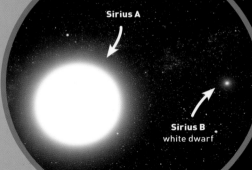

Sirius A

Sirius B
white dwarf

ALPHA CENTAURI: MULTI-STAR SYSTEM

> The nearest star to Earth, other than the Sun, Alpha Centauri is 'only' 4.2 light years away.
> It is the third-brightest star in the sky.
> It is a multi-star system consisting of three stars: Alpha Centauri A, Alpha Centauri B and Alpha Centauri C.

Alpha Centauri A and B

ALGOL: BLINKING DEMON STAR

> Algol is a bright triple star that looks like a binary star from Earth, but has another faint companion.
> Its brightness changes, so it is called the blinking star.
> It is about 93 light years from Earth.
> Find it in the constellation of Perseus.

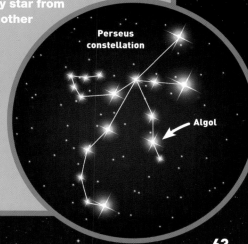

Perseus constellation

Algol

EXOPLANETS

An exoplanet is a planet orbiting a star beyond our solar system. So far, more than 4,000 exoplanets have been discovered in other galaxies. Scientists believe that every star in the universe may have an exoplanet. Some of these rocky planets are Earth-sized while others are much bigger super-Earths.

LOOKING FOR EXOPLANETS

The Kepler Space Telescope is on the lookout for other planets in the Milky Way. So far, more than 30 have been found at the 'right' distance from their star, where liquid water is possible.

The James Webb Space Telescope is a massive new telescope that may be able to explore distant exoplanets. It will take over from the Hubble Space Telescope, which has taken some of the most amazing space photographs up until now. The James Webb Telescope will be able to make even more extraordinary discoveries possible in deep space.

The Kepler Space Telescope

4,000-PLUS EXOPLANETS

51 Pegasi was the first star found to have an orbiting planet. This first exoplanet, the size of Jupiter, was discovered in 1995. Since then, thousands more have been found in all shapes and sizes. They are common in our galaxy and new discoveries are made each year.

Exoplanet

Star

DID YOU KNOW?

Scientists think there could be billions of Earth-size planets within the Milky Way galaxy alone. One of the problems is that exoplanets are difficult to see, even with telescopes, as they are hidden by the brightness of the stars that they orbit.

THE STARS
SUPERNOVA!

A supernova is the massive explosion of a dying star. Supernovae can outshine whole galaxies and give out more energy than our Sun will in its entire lifetime. These events create all the heavy metals, such as iron and gold, that exist in the universe.

HOW LONG DOES IT TAKE?

Stars take a few million years to die, then in less than a second, a star can collapse, sending out massive galactic shockwaves. It brightens in a few months and then just takes years to fade away. One of the most famous leftover supernovae is Crab Nebula (or M1), which is 10 light years across. It was first spotted by Chinese astronomers in 1054 and has been eyed up by astronomers ever since. The star is still dying and so the supernova is still growing.

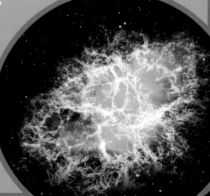

Crab nebula

MAKING ATOMS

The first atoms were made 380,000 years after the Big Bang, the moment when the universe formed. These atoms and every atom ever since were made in the stars. As the stars die, they explode in a burst of gas and dust. This dust and gas thrown out into space forms all the stuff or 'matter' that exists in the universe.

GOLD DUST

When really big stars explode and die or when two stars crash, they make heavy metals such as gold. Gold dust is then hurled out across the universe. About 3.9 billion years ago, Earth was bombarded by meteorites full of gold. This gold sank down into the centre of the Earth towards the planet's iron core.

ASTRONOMY

Astronomy is the study of the cosmos: the planets, stars, asteroids, comets and the galaxies in space. From studying stars to understanding space to teaching and inventing, there are lots of ways to be an astronomer if you are star crazy!

STAR MAPPING

As long ago as 1000BC, the Babylonians were mapping the sky. Greeks, Romans and many others joined these sparkly dots to draw familiar patterns of stars in the night sky. This helped astronomers find particular stars or galaxies and learn about the cosmos. It also helped them track time, which was useful for farming, timing their religious ceremonies and getting around.

FINDING THE WAY

Early humans probably stared at the stars to track their path. The bright North Star, Polaris, points north and familiar patterns of other stars helped travellers and sailors map their way across land and sea.

Where to find Polaris, North Star

TAKE A LOOK

Today everyone from space scientists to school children can explore the skies in different ways. From using giant telescopes in observatories to mobile phone Apps in your garden, people on Earth are looking up and learning about their place in space.

THE STARS
CONSTELLATIONS

Astronomers have divided the sky up into 88 areas or 'constellations'. Within each constellation there is a named group of stars, which look from Earth as if they make up shapes in the sky. This makes them easy to recognise, observe and study. In fact, stars are randomly dotted in space.

The Orion constellation

DID YOU KNOW?

You see different constellations depending on whether you are stargazing in the southern or the northern hemisphere.

Orion: the 'Hunter'

Find Orion's belt of three bright stars in the middle of the constellation, and the star Betelgeuse in his armpit. Can be seen from both hemispheres.

Canis Major: the 'Big Dog'

This constellation can be seen in both hemispheres at different times. It contains Sirius, or dog star. Sirius is one of the closest stars to Earth.

Sirius

Ursa Major: the 'Big Dipper'

The Big Dipper, also known as the Plough, is a really easy constellation to spot. You can find it in summer in the northernmost part of the sky.

Ursa Minor: the 'Little Dipper'

Ursa is Latin for 'bear', and this is the little one. Spot the North Star, Polaris, shining at the tip of this constellation, which lies in the northern sky.

Polaris

Pegasus: the 'Winged Horse'

This constellation is famous for hosting the first exoplanet (planet outside the solar system) found around a normal star.

Draco: the 'Dragon'

Seen in the northern hemisphere this is one of the largest constellations. It snakes its way across the sky like a serpent, or dragon.

Hercules: the 'Hero'

The figure is usually drawn with his foot on the head of Draco, which is appropriate as one of the labours of Hercules was to slay a dragon.

Cygnus: the 'Swan'

Cygnus is large and easy to spot. The Milky Way passes through the middle of the cross, littering it with the richest star fields in the northern sky.

TWINKLE TWINKLE

If you look hard on a clear night you might see 2,000 stars scattered across the night sky. These stars appear to twinkle, although in fact this isn't the case. It is only viewing them through Earth's atmosphere that makes them sparkle.

ANCIENT LIGHT

Light from stars takes a long time to reach Earth. Some stars we can see are already dead, we can still see them because their light has taken so long to reach us. The visible energy waves travel at the speed of light ... 300,000 kilometres per second! The star designated as HD 140283 is currently the oldest known star in the galaxy. It is called the Methuselah star after a story in the Bible of a man who lived for 969 years.

Methuselah star

THE ZODIAC

The Zodiac is an area of sky that maps the Sun's path over a year. In the Zodiac, there are 12 groups of stars. Some people believe that there is a link between these groups of stars and people's lives on Earth, which is called astrology. Unlike astronomy, astrology is not a science.

> **Capricornus 'Sea goat'** — 22 December – 19 January
> **Aquarius 'Water bearer'** — 20 January – 18 February
> **Pisces 'Fishes'** — 19 February – 20 March
> **Aries 'Ram'** — 21 March – 19 April
> **Taurus 'Bull'** — 20 April – 20 May
> **Gemini 'The Twins'** — 21 May – 20 June
> **Cancer 'Crab'** — 21 June – 22 July
> **Leo 'Lion'** — 23 July – 22 August
> **Virgo 'Virgin'** — 23 August – 22 September
> **Libra 'Scales'** — 23 September – 22 October
> **Scorpius 'Scorpion'** — 23 October – 21 November
> **Sagittarius 'Archer'** — 22 November – 21 December
> **Ophiuchus 'Snake Bearer'** — Not used in astrology

WHO FOUND THEM?

The Zodiac constellations were found by the Babylonians, who passed their knowledge on to the ancient Greeks, who then told the Romans, and now we recognise these constellations in the sky.

Leo 'Lion' is one of the few Zodiac constellations that actually resembles its name. The Gemini twins looks like two stick figures with outstretched arms touching.

Leo the Lion

PISCES

ARIES

AQUARIUS

TAURUS

CAPRICORN

GEMINI

SAGITTARIUS

CANCER

SCORPIO

LEO

LIBRA

VIRGO

THE STARS
STARGAZERS

HANS LIPPERSHEY

Hans Lippershey (1570–1619)
This glasses maker from the
Netherlands invented the
lens that made it possible
to see things that were far
away as if they were close up.
It is likely that he invented the
telescope that Galileo later improved.

ISAAC NEWTON

Isaac Newton (1642–1727) An Englishman
who discovered the laws of gravity, the
natural force that pulls everything
together in the universe. The Sun's
gravity pulls Earth and all the other
planets around it. Without the pull
of gravity, we would drift off into
space. Newton also invented the
type of telescope that is widely
used today to look up at the stars.

EJNAR HERTZSPRUNG

Ejnar Hertzsprung (1873–1967)
This Danish astronomer was famous
for working out how the brightness
of a star related to its colour.

HENRY RUSSELL

Henry Russell (1877–1957) An
American astrophysicist who was
interested in how stars evolved.
With Hertzsprung, he created the
famous H–R diagram (see page 58)
that maps the stars according to
brightness and temperature.

DAME JOCELYN BELL BURNELL

Dame Jocelyn Bell Burnell (1943–)
A British scientist from Northern
Ireland who discovered a new kind
of star. She found stars whose
light changed between strong and
weak light ... it 'pulsed'. These
stars are called 'pulsars'.

GALAXIES

Galaxies are sculpted by gravity into gigantic shapes and clusters. Consisting of empty space, scattered with stars and planets, they spin into infinity.

WHAT IS A GALAXY?

Galaxies are great gatherings of stars and clouds of space dust, swirling across space. They are made of trillions of stars held together by gravity and strange, mysterious stuff called dark matter. In the middle of almost every galaxy is a vortex of gravity called a supermassive black hole.

**M101
Pinwheel galaxy**

HOW MANY?

Of course, nobody really knows how many galaxies there are but giant telescopes are always seeking to discover more. Some are found in pairs, some in clusters and others gather in superclusters. Galaxies don't have edges, and are constantly spinning and moving across space. Sizes of galaxies and the distances they travel are almost impossible to imagine and even more difficult to measure.

EMPTY SPACES

Between the stars there is plenty of empty space, with floating clouds of dust and gas, where new stars are born. Around these new stars dust spins and clumps into planets, asteroids, meteorites and comets, all hurled around by gravity.

M78

THE 'M' IN GALAXY NAMING

Galaxies are named with the letter M and a number after a French astronomer called Charles Messier (1730–1817). He published a catalogue of 110 'objects' in space that can be seen from the northern hemisphere. They are named and numbered after him, using the M of his name; 42 of them are galaxies.

M104
Sombrero galaxy

GALAXY SHAPES

Galaxies spin in lots of shapes but most are spiral, barred or elliptical. Others are shapeless blurs of stars. Our galaxy is called the Milky Way. A closer look at our milky blur shows its spiral shape, with a flat spinning disc in the middle and arches of stars curving outwards into space.

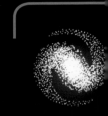

Elliptical

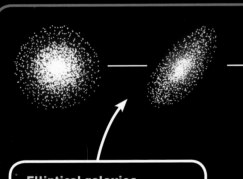

Elliptical galaxies

Largely composed of older mature stars. These types seldom have star forming areas.

Spiral

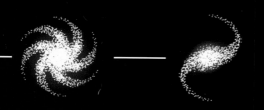

Irregular galaxies

These galaxies are often small and don't have enough gravitational force to organise into a more regular form.

Irregular

Barred spiral

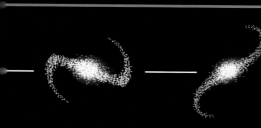

 **FOCUS ON** # GALAXIES

THE MILKY WAY: OUR GALAXY

- The Milky Way is a spiral galaxy.
- It consists of more than 100 billion stars.
- It contains our solar system, far out on a cosmic arm, 25,000 light years from the central black hole.
- More than half of the stars are older than the 4.5-billion-year-old Sun.
- Most of the galaxy looks blue, with a red centre.

Milky Way

ANDROMEDA: A SPIRAL GALAXY

- Andromeda (M31) is a spiral galaxy.
- It is a giant galaxy, much bigger than the Milky Way, containing a trillion stars.
- It is the closest galaxy to our own Milky Way, 2.5 million light years from Earth.

Andromeda

M49: AN ELLIPTICAL GALAXY

> This was the first galaxy discovered by Charles Messier in 1777.
> Elliptical galaxies are slower-spinning and have a stretched-out lozenge shape. They spin in red, the colour of the older stars.
> There are no cold clouds of gas where new stars can form.
> It's in the Virgo group of stars.

M49

M95: A BARRED GALAXY

> This galaxy has a stretched spiral shape with spinning arms at each end of a bar.
> It is 33 million light years away.
> It sparkles with the light of young blue stars.
> It belongs to the Leo group of stars.

M95

GALAXIES
THE BIG CRASH

The universe is expanding, so galaxies are moving outwards towards infinity. The further away they are, the faster they are moving. They often collide, in which case they either just pass through each other (because there's so much empty space) or they crash and form a giant galactic merger.

THE BIG SMASH

Andromeda and the Milky Way are moving towards each other at 400 kilometres per hour. In about 4 billion years, the two galaxies will crash into each other. The timing of this monster collision has been predicted by Europe's Gaia spacecraft. No one knows what kind of crash it will be but it is certain to light up the night sky for any life on Earth that is around to watch!

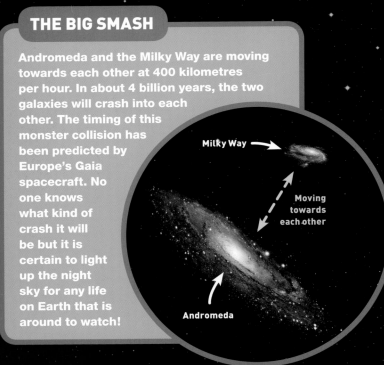

Milky Way

Moving towards each other

Andromeda

CRASHES...

Long before the Andromeda and Milky Way crash, there may be another galactic merger: the Milky Way will collide with its neighbouring galaxy, the Large Magellanic Cloud, in about 2.5 billion years. This violent collision will be far from Earth and it's unlikely that our planet will feel the impact.

Large Magellanic Cloud

Milky Way

... AND COLLISIONS

The collision between the Antennae galaxies, which are located about 62 million light years from Earth, began more than 100 million years ago and is still occurring. During the merger, 100 trillion Suns' worth of material collide, mix and ignite. These two massive structures, each 100,000 light years across, host hundreds of billions of stars.

Antennae galaxies

NEBULAE

The spaces between the stars, where dust and gas gather, are called nebulae. These gigantic masses of colour form cosmic shapes that scientists can recognise and name. They glitter and glow in bright blue and red gas. Some in deep space have been photographed by the Hubble Space Telescope and the Spitzer Space Telescope.

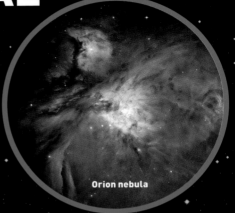

Orion nebula

SPACE FOR BIRTH AND DEATH

Some nebulae are places where new stars are born, in which case they are called 'star nurseries'. Other nebulae form when giant stars go supernova – that is they explode and die. The Carina Nebula is 8,500 light years away Earth.

Carina nebula

Crab nebula

The remains of a supernova in the constellation of Taurus. It is 6,500 light years from Earth. A rapidly spinning neutron star is embedded in the centre of the Crab nebula.

Horse head nebula

1,500 light years from Earth. Bright spots in the Horsehead nebula's base are young stars just in the process of forming.

Eagle nebula

7,000 light years from Earth. There is an active star-forming region within the nebula, known as the Pillars of Creation, which contains proto-stars.

Butterfly nebula

A complicated nebula 4,000 light years from Earth. The bright clusters and nebulae of our night sky are often given names from nature.

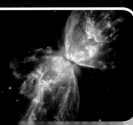

GALACTIC SPIN

Like all galaxies, the Milky Way is always spinning and we are spinning with it. Scientists have discovered that all galaxies, whatever size they are, spin a full turn once every billion years. If galaxies didn't spin they would collapse inwards into the supermassive black holes in the middle.

Here we are

The Milky Way is our home galaxy in the universe and home to 400 billion stars as well as our own Sun and solar system. Our solar system is far out on the Orion Spur of the spiral-shaped Milky Way galaxy. The Milky Way, along with everything else in the universe, is moving through space. The Earth moves around the Sun, the Sun around the Milky Way,

120,000–180,000 light-years in diameter

Sun

Orion Spur

Perseus arm

Outer arm

DID YOU KNOW?

We don't have a picture of the entire Milky Way as we are inside it. The galactic disk, about 26,000 light years from the galactic centre. It would be like trying to take a picture of your own house from the inside.

Supermassive black hole called Sagittarius A*

Milky Way spin

Our galaxy spins really slowly. It 'only' takes about 220 million years for our solar system to make a complete orbit of the Milky Way, so one galactic turn ago, dinosaurs ruled the Earth. There have only been 20 galactic turns of the Milky Way since our solar system was formed. The gas and dust in our galaxy is rotating at around 270 kilometres per second.

DIRECTION OF SPIN

BLACK HOLES

Black holes are not really holes. They are objects in space where gravity is so strong that even light gets bent and sucked in. Space telescopes show what happens to light and stars around a black hole, so we know they are out there. Nothing can ever escape from a black hole.

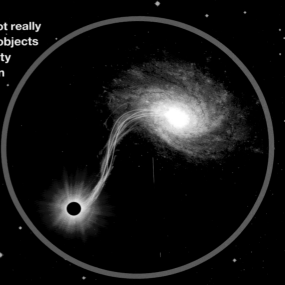

DID YOU KNOW?

If you were to fall into a black hole (which you won't), you would be 'spaghettified'. This means that the forces of gravity in the black hole would stretch you out into thin spaghetti-like strips.

BLACK HOLE FACTS

> Some black holes formed after the Big Bang and others form when stars die.

> There are black holes of many different sizes all over the universe.

> All galaxies swirl around a black hole, some of which are supermassive.

> The supermassive black hole at the centre of the Milky Way galaxy is called Sagittarius A.

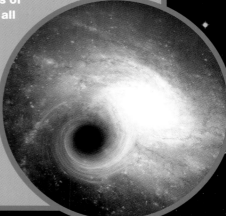

ON CAMERA

In an exciting scientific breakthrough, a black hole was photographed for the first time in 2019. It was a black hole that is 55 million light years away from Earth and is at the centre of a galaxy called M87.

GALAXIES

GALAXY SPOTTERS

THOMAS WRIGHT

Thomas Wright (1711–1786) An Englishman who first described the Milky Way. He realised that Earth and humans are not really very important relative to the scale of a vast universe.

CHARLES MESSIER

Charles Messier (1730–1817) A French astronomer who made a list of 110 blurry light objects in the sky. He made the list because he wanted to tell the difference between comets and these other objects, which were clusters of stars and nebulae.

EDWIN HUBBLE

Edwin Hubble (1889–1953) An American who discovered a way of grouping galaxies and worked out that the universe is expanding. The Hubble Space Telescope named after him is about the size of a school bus. It takes pictures of stars and galaxies in deep space.

JAMES WEBB

James Webb (1906–1992) An American who ran the American space agency NASA and after whom the new James Webb Space Telescope is named.

James Webb Space Telescope

THE UNIVERSE

The universe is an unimaginably big, cold, dark, empty space but it is also full of wonder and mystery. Understanding it is critical to understanding ourselves.

THE BIG BANG

Space and time started with a Big Bang. Nobody knows if anything existed before the Big Bang or what triggered this massive cosmic explosion. What we do know is that this split second when the universe began happened about 13.8 billion years ago.

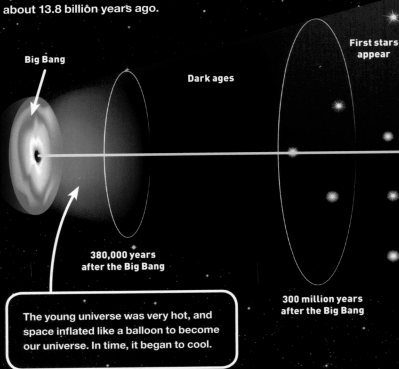

Big Bang

Dark ages

First stars appear

380,000 years after the Big Bang

300 million years after the Big Bang

The young universe was very hot, and space inflated like a balloon to become our universe. In time, it began to cool.

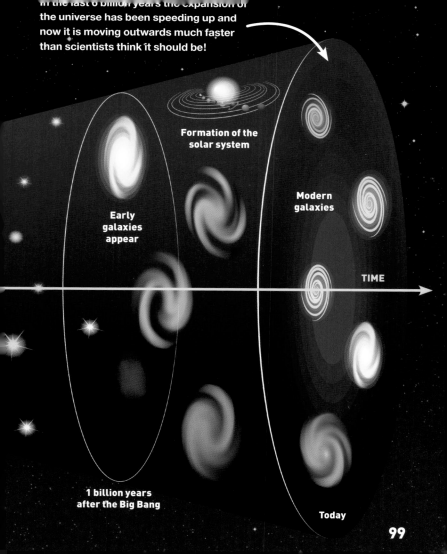

In the last 6 billion years the expansion of the universe has been speeding up and now it is moving outwards much faster than scientists think it should be!

Formation of the solar system

Early galaxies appear

Modern galaxies

TIME

1 billion years after the Big Bang

Today

99

THE UNIVERSE
A QUIET BEGINNING

The name Big Bang is misleading: it wasn't a 'big bang' at all because space is a vacuum that sound waves can't pass through. So, space is in fact quiet. The term 'Big Bang' was first used on the radio by an astronomer who didn't believe in the event – he thought the universe had always existed. He was later proved wrong when scientists discovered evidence for the beginning of the universe, but the name Big Bang stuck.

AFTERGLOW

The evidence for the Big Bang was the discovery of cosmic microwaves in the universe. This is because the Big Bang created lots of energy and, over time, these energy waves stretched into long microwaves as the universe expanded. This afterglow from the Big Bang is everywhere in the universe – it is all around you! It is called Cosmic Background Radiation (CMR) and is evidence that there was a moment, the Big Bang, when the universe began.

EVER-EXPANDING

Since it formed, the universe has been expanding. The thing pushing the universe apart is a mysterious force called dark energy. The space between galaxies is stretching and pushing those galaxies apart. The expansion of the universe was discovered by an astronomer called Edwin Hubble. His revelation helped scientists work out how old the universe is.

The universe continues to expand like a balloon

DID YOU KNOW?

Scientists think it would take 46 billion light years to get to the 'edge' of the universe that humans can see... With a lot of help from telescopes and technology!

SPACETIME

Before the Big Bang there was no time and no space. Scientists, from Einstein onwards, discovered that space and time are actually the same thing. This is 'spacetime'. Spacetime may be infinite and flat – something that's very difficult for us humans to imagine! The physics genius Einstein came up with two theories in the 1900s, which explain spacetime. One is the Theory of Special Relativity and the other is the Theory of General Relativity.

THE THEORY OF GENERAL RELATIVITY

The Theory of General Relativity explains gravity and states that spacetime is like a trampoline. It says that when things like planets and stars move in spacetime, they create ripples. These curves are gravity, the force that explains why things fall when you drop them.

THE THEORY OF SPECIAL RELATIVITY

The Theory of Special Relativity says that movement is relative. The movement of one thing is always relative to the movement of another. Special Relativity also explains that light always travels at the same speed: 300,000 kilometres per second. The Theory of Special Relativity says that space and time are connected – this is spacetime. Spacetime bends around big things, such as planets and stars.

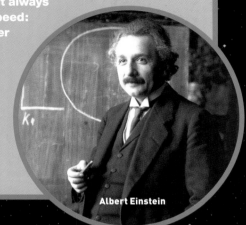

Albert Einstein

DID YOU KNOW?

The speed of light is a cosmic speed limit. It is the fastest speed possible in the universe. It is impossible for humans to travel at the speed of light. But guess what? If you could travel at the speed of light you could go round the world 7.5 times in a second!

THE UNIVERSE
FORCES OF NATURE

There are four Fundamental Forces of Nature, without which the universe would fall apart. These forces rule the way everything in the universe works. They are gravity, electromagnetism, and the strong and weak nuclear forces.

1. GRAVITY

Gravity pulls everything in the universe together. This force pulls the planets around the Sun in our solar system and it pulls us down to Earth so that we don't float off into space. In supermassive black holes at the centre of galaxies, gravity is super strong. In other places in the universe, it is really weak. If you step on the Moon you feel light and bounce around because gravity on the Moon is weak.

DID YOU KNOW?

Gravity is the weakest of the four Fundamental Forces of Nature.

2. WEAK NUCLEAR FORCE

Weak nuclear forces work inside atoms.

3. ELECTROMAGNETISM

Electromagnetic force is much stronger than gravity. It combines electric and magnetic forces. It is the glue holding all the atoms in the universe together.

Auroras are electromagnetic light shows

An aurora borealis seen from space

4. STRONG NUCLEAR FORCE

The strong interaction is very strong, but very short-ranged. It is responsible for holding the nuclei of atoms together.

THE UNIVERSE
LIGHT IN SPACE

L ight is a type of energy wave that is visible, although humans can only see a tiny part of all the energy waves that exist in the universe. We see the 'visible spectrum', which includes all the colours of the rainbow. There are also all sorts of rays of energy that we cannot see but that we know exist in the universe. These are: gamma rays, X-rays, ultraviolet and infrared light, microwaves and radio waves. Each of these different energy waves are different lengths and they travel at different speeds.

Electromagnetic spectrum

This shows the different waves of energy in order of wavelength from the longest to the shortest. All electromagnetic waves travel at the speed of light in a vacuum like space. Visible light can be seen in the middle of the spectrum.

Infrared light

Infrared light is given out by cosmic dust and stars that are warmer than the cold emptiness of space – but not hot enough to glow with light that we can see. Astronomers use special infrared cameras to find and study cooler objects in space, such as red stars, which shine in infrared.

INFRARED

MICROWAVE

RADIO

WAVES IN SPACE

Astronomers use special kinds of telescopes and cameras to search for these different energy waves in space. They find objects in the universe that emit these energy waves and then they can learn about them.

Pleiades star cluster in infrared light

Ultraviolet light (UV)

Hot objects, like the Sun, give out UV, a light wave that we cannot see. Luckily, our atmosphere blocks out most of these powerful rays, which can damage life on Earth. Really hot stars give out more ultraviolet light.

X-rays

X-rays have lots of energy. They are created in extreme environments like black holes, exploding stars and crashing galaxies.

Sun seen in x-rays

Gamma rays

These are super energetic energy waves created in the most massive star explosions of all.

UV

X-RAY

GAMMA

ENERGY

WILL IT ALL END?

Nobody knows how big the universe is. It may be infinite ... but this idea is impossible to prove! Scientists have worked out how the universe began, but nobody knows if or how it will end.

1. BIG RIP

There could be a Big Rip in which everything in the universe is eventually torn apart.

2. BIG CRUNCH

Or a Big Crunch in which the universe collapses into an immensely massive black hole.

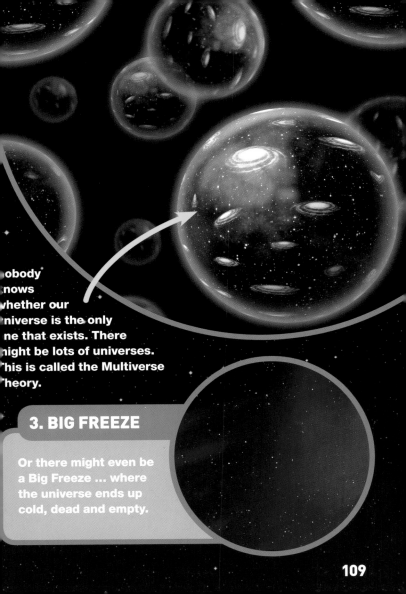

Nobody knows whether our universe is the only one that exists. There might be lots of universes. This is called the Multiverse Theory.

3. BIG FREEZE

Or there might even be a Big Freeze ... where the universe ends up cold, dead and empty.

SCIENTISTS

OLE RØMER

Ole Rømer (1644–1710) This Danish astronomer was the first person to measure the speed of light. Now we know that all energy in the universe travels at the speed of light.

ALBERT EINSTEIN

Einstein (1879–1955) A German physicist who developed two Theories of Relativity (see page 102), which help to explain how the universe works. He explained gravity and worked out that space and time are actually the same thing. He called it 'spacetime'.

MAGGIE ADERIN-POCOCK

Maggie Aderin-Pocock (1968–) A popular British space engineer, scientist and TV presenter who enthuses children and adults alike about the wonders of the universe. She set up her own companies, which tour schools to talk about the universe. She dreamed of going into space as a child.

ROBERT WOODROW WILSON AND ARNO PENZIAS

Robert Woodrow Wilson (1936–) and Arno Penzias (1933–) Astronomers who discovered Cosmic Background Radiation through the Holmdel Horn Antenna. These cosmic microwaves in the universe prove the theory of the universe beginning with the Big Bang (see page 98).

Wilson and Penzias and the Holmdel Horn Antenna

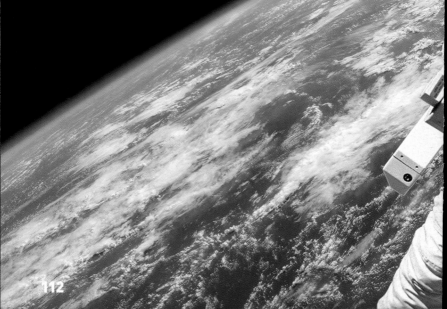

SPACE MYSTERIES

Many scientists believe we are entering a new Space Age of discovery and understanding of the place we call space. Here are some of the biggest mysteries that scientists are trying to unravel...

SPACE MYSTERIES

SPACE AGENCIES

There are a growing number of space agencies around the world searching for answers to fascinating space mysteri Some of the biggest space agency teams are located in North America, China, Russia, Japan and India. There's also the European Space Agency, which is formed of more than 20 countries, and the Asia Pacific Space Cooperation.

WHAT DO THEY DO?

International space agencies work together to peacefully explore space. They use the latest science and technology to find out more about Earth, our solar system and the universe. From medicine and materials to monitoring our climate and water quality, space science also benefits our life on Earth.

SPACE LAW

All countries going into space agree to help each other rescue astronauts, share information about dangers in outer space, take responsibility for damage of objects in space, and behave in a way that protects space and everybody who works there.

Space walking

COUNTRIES WITH SPACE AGENCIES

Algeria, Australia, Brazil, Canada, China, Denmark, France, Germany, India, Israel, Italy, Japan, Kenya, Luxembourg, Mexico, New Zealand, Norway, Pakistan, Peru, Republic of Korea, Romania, Russian Federation, South Africa, Spain, Ukraine, United Arab Emirates, United Kingdom, United States of America.

The Russian Soyuz spacecraft

SPACE MYSTERIES
IN THE DARK

One of the biggest mysteries of space is dark energy. After the Big Bang, the universe was pushed apart by a strange, all-powerful force. This force is dark energy, and scientists think it makes up most of the universe – more than 68 per cent. It is everywhere, still pushing everything in the universe apart at a faster and faster rate.

Scientists have learned about dark energy by studying the expansion of the universe and looking at how fast galaxies are moving apart. But it is one of the biggest mysteries of the cosmos because they know what it does but they don't know what it is.

A SPEEDY SURPRISE

Dark energy was discovered in the 1990s by astronomers who worked out that the expansion of the universe is accelerating rather than slowing down. This was a big surprise to space scientists. By studying exploding stars with the Hubble and other space telescopes, they found the first evidence of dark energy.

Exploding stars light research into dark energy

DARK MATTER

Dark matter is an invisible web of mysterious 'stuff' that holds galaxies, and everything else in the universe, together. No one knows what it is. Scientists only really know it exists because gravity alone is not strong enough to hold galaxies together. Dark matter is pulling stars around in swirling galaxies across the universe. It is thought to make up about 27 per cent of the universe.

WHY ARE THEY DARK?

We call dark energy and dark matter 'dark' because we humans cannot see them. Scientists believe they exist because they help explain how they think the universe works. We can see other matter in the universe, such as stars and planets and life on Earth – yet these visible objects make up only 5 per cent of the universe.

SPACE MYSTERIES
WORMHOLES

No-one has ever seen or found a wormhole but scientists believe that they exist. Wormholes are believed to be like bridges across time and space in the universe or maybe portals to another universe.

TIME SHORT CUTS

Wormholes are thought to be hollow tunnels that cross from one part of the universe to another. The time taken to pass through this tunnel would be much less than it would take to travel through normal space. This means you could travel faster than the speed of light through a wormhole.

THE CHALLENGE

A wormhole is a very dangerous place. It would probably collapse before you got a chance to travel from one end to the other.

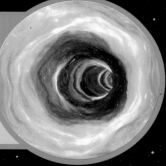

Earth

Wormhole

Hyperspace

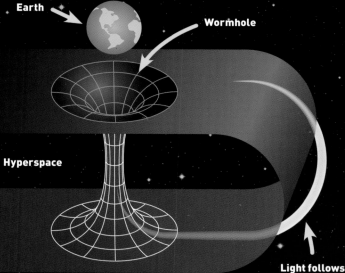

Light follows the curvature of spacetime

Distant galaxy

SPACE MYSTERIES
LOOKING FOR LIFE

Life on our planet exists in the strangest extreme places – from frozen deserts to acidic lakes, in superheated water and in rocks deep down in the Earth. In an infinite universe, it is unlikely that life only exists on planet Earth.

DIFFERENT KINDS OF LIFE

Space scientists are looking at places where there might have been some form of life in the past, perhaps when water existed on Mars. They are also looking for evidence of tiny forms of microbial life living in extreme conditions, perhaps in the underground oceans on Jupiter's moon Europa. And they are particularly on the lookout for signs of intelligent life in interstellar space, perhaps on a distant planet in a distant solar system.

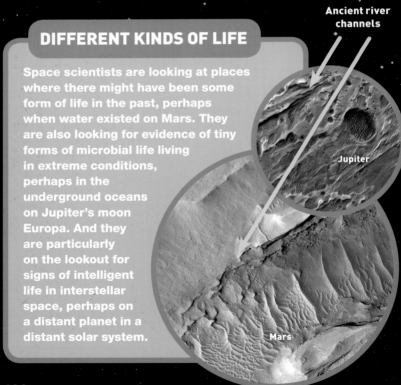

Ancient river channels

Jupiter

Mars

GOLDILOCKS ZONE

Earth orbits in the 'Goldilocks Zone' – just the right distance from the Sun for life to be possible. Water is needed for life as we know it, and to have surface water, planets must be just the right distance from the star they are orbiting. Too close and it will evaporate; too far away and it will freeze. So, scientists are on the lookout for planets and moons orbiting in the Goldilocks Zone around a star.

The Goldilocks Zone where the temperature is 'just right'

Star

Hot

Cold

DID YOU KNOW?

There is a special maths equation called the Drake Equation that calculates the chances of finding other life in the universe. It turns out that there's a pretty high chance! It was worked out in 1964, but no alien life has been found since then, yet...

ALIEN LIFE

LIFE ON MARS

Scientists have been looking for signs of life on Mars for a long time. Though they have found evidence of liquid water, there are still no signs of life.

Surface of Mars

JUPITER'S MOONS

Jupiter's moon Europa has a buried ocean of liquid water.

Surface of Europa

SATURN'S MOONS

Saturn's moon Enceladus has buried oceans of water and many of the other ingredients required for life.

Enceladus

FURTHER OUT

Super-Earth exoplanet LHS 1140b is just one of the distant exoplanets in the Goldilocks Zone of its faint red star. This means that it's not too hot and not too cold, so the conditions could be right for life. But this massive planet is 40 light years away!

DID YOU KNOW?

Life on Earth probably began in deep, hot water where atoms of carbon, nitrogen, hydrogen, sulphur and phosphorous got together. It happened at the right time in the right place, and involved a lot of luck.

ALIEN NOISES

If life is discovered elsewhere in the universe it is unlikely to look like life on Earth. It may be intelligent like us or it may be just a hot soup of bubbling bacteria. If it is intelligent, it may recognise sound and so scientists have set up radio telescopes to act as giant ears on Earth, listening for noise signals from alien forms of life. So far there is a deafening silence from deep space.

Radio telescope

DID YOU KNOW?

Spacecraft *Voyager 1* took 33 years to reach the edge of the solar system. It's now heading into interstellar space.

GOLDEN RECORD

In addition to using
radio telescopes to
listen from Earth, space
robots carry messages
from people on Earth
into space – in the hope
that intelligent alien life
will find and respond to our
friendly hello! In 1977, a Golden
Record was sent into space on
Voyager 1, which is now 21 billion kilometres
from Earth on a voyage into deep space.

WHAT'S ON IT?

The Golden Record contains
116 pictures of life on Earth,
greetings from people
in 55 languages, and a
huge array of sounds
– from whale songs
to thunder as well as
music and a message
from the 39th American
President Carter and the
United Nations.

SPACE MYSTERIES
DISCOVERERS

VERA RUBIN

Vera Rubin (1928–2016) An astronomer famous for studying the spinning galaxies and providing evidence that most of the universe was made of dark matter.

ARTHUR C CLARKE

Arthur C Clarke (1917–2008) Science fiction writer best known for writing the script and novel *2001: A Space Odyssey*. He made many popular films and became famous for his surprisingly accurate 'space predictions'.

CARL SAGAN

Carl Sagan (1934–1996) Cosmologist and scientist famous for looking for extraterrestrial life in the universe and making astronomy popular, writing books and appearing on TV space shows.

STEPHEN HAWKING

Stephen Hawking (1942–2018) Author and physicist famous for his work unravelling the mysteries of black holes and making complicated space science easier for people to understand. His book *A Brief History of Time* appeared on the *Sunday Times* best-seller list for a record-breaking 237 weeks.

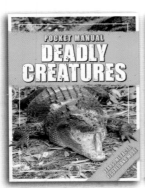
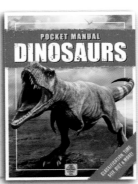
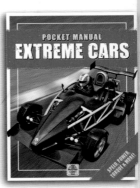